The best mates guide to...

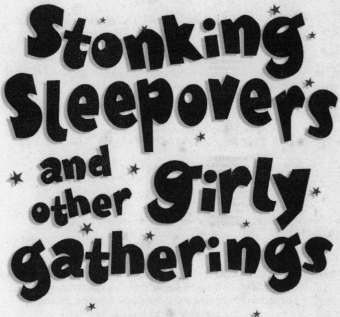

Stonking
Sleepovers
and other Girly
gatherings

★ Gill Sutherland ★

Scholastic Children's Books
Commonwealth House, 1–19 New Oxford Street,
London, WC1A 1NU, UK
A division of Scholastic Ltd
London ~ New York ~ Toronto ~ Sydney ~ Auckland
Mexico City ~ New Delhi ~ Hong Kong

Published in the UK by Scholastic Ltd, 2003
Text copyright © Gill Sutherland, 2003
Illustrations copyright © Kirstie Aitken, 2003

ISBN 0 439 97826 2

Printed and bound by Nørhaven Paperback A/S, Denmark

2 4 6 8 10 9 7 5 3 1

The right of Gill Sutherland and Kirstie Aitken to be identified as the author
and illustrator of this work respectively has been asserted
by them in accordance with the Copyright, Designs and
Patents Act, 1988.

Contents

⭐ Want to be Mates? ⭐

Hi! I'm Molly White, aka The Author, and am
I pleased to meet you! Just so you know,
I'm a diplomatic Libra, share my mum and
dad with my incredibly dim and annoying
twin bro Billy and live in a sort of urban sprawl we'll
call Dullsville, Spamshire. Naturally, I'm gorgeous to
behold and something of a genius in the brain stakes.
(OK, really I'm a bit short, prone to spots, have sticky-out
hair that no amount of conditioner will pummel into a
glossy sheen and my teachers reckon I'm "easily
distracted" and "lazy". Pah!) I like long words, chocolate,
art, saving the planet, cheese puffs, poetry, most music,
wise people and, of course, sleepover parties! I do *not*
like fools, pollution or broccoli (bleurrrgh! the evil weed).

But that's enough about me. I've heard that you're
here for brilliant tips and ideas about how to put on the
best sleepover or girly gathering EVER. Well you've
definitely come to the right place, 'cos me and the
gang are here to help… So come on – it's time to meet
your new Best Mates!

⭐

Flower

AKA: Flower Spirit Delaney (hello, hippy parents!)

Star sign: Dreamy Pisces

Likes: "Animals, wildlife and my mum teaching me about aromatherapy, feng shui and other new-age stuff."

Dislikes: "Nothing. I like *everything*!"

Sleepovers held: "A couple – for my last one I did a loved-up theme for Valentine's – with heart-shaped pizza and soppy videos. Me and the Mates also made tons of glittery Valentine's cards and sent them out anonymously at school!"

Missy

AKA: Nora Baxter (don't call her that though, she gets annoyed…)

Star sign: Crabby Cancer

Likes: "I'm heavily into R&B and garage and I love urban clothes. Plus, you'll never see me without my moby!"

Dislikes: "Um, being without my phone – like in class, boo!"

Sleepovers held: "People crash at my place all the time, so dunno … at a guess, like, ten a year."

6

Bubble

AKA: Cybil Bubridge (but no one calls her Cybil, not even her mum)

Star sign: Adventurous Aquarius

Likes: "Mega-loud rawk music, running, having a laugh with my mates, playing pranks, world travel and FOOOOD (lots of it)!!!"

Dislikes: "Wusses and dresses. Oh, and being tall and gangly."

Sleepovers held: "I'm what you'd call a very experienced, erm, guest – it's hassle-free and you just get on with enjoying yourself!"

Princess

AKA: Pandora Moxbury (now does that sound posh, or does that sound posh?)

Star sign: Sophisticated Aries

Likes: "I adore clothes, shopping, fashion magazines and interior design."

Dislikes: "Bad-hair days and having no money to spend."

Sleepovers held: "Tons! I love being the hostess with the mostest – whether it's a birthday, Easter, Halloween, or 'cos it's the weekend – any excuse will do!"

Impressed so far? I hope so, because together we Best Mates have heaps of incredible ideas, awesome advice and terrific tips to make sure you put on the Best Sleepover in the world! Stick with us and you'll find out how to:

★ Win your parents over with our sneaky wheedling advice!

★ Lay perfect painless plans for a perfect party!

★ Banish your niggly worries with the coolest problem page in the cosmos!

What's more, you can do our quiz to find out what sort of sleepover girl YOU are. And, as you're officially now our New Best Mate, we offer up the following guarantee of true friendship:

The Best Mates' pledge

1. To be on hand with our expert advice 24/7, sleeping by your side if necessary.

★

2. To never get the hump with you – even if you completely ignore our advice.

★

3. To ~~never~~ hardly ever snigger at your many, many mistakes, mad fads and truly bonkers brainwaves.

★

4. Basically, you have our undying love, loyalty blah de blah de blah and can borrow any of our things, any time ... for eternity!

Right, enough of that business – your sleepover's not going to organize itself, Mate. So, let's get down to some serious preparation...

Getting Started

So, you've decided to host a sleepover – congratulations! You are in for a fantastic time! OK, let's start with the most basic question in the world: WHAT IS A SLEEPOVER? Princess, oh Queen of Sleepovers, perhaps you can answer that one?

❝Easy. A sleepover is when you have a group of friends over to stay the night. You do stuff like play games, watch videos, munch on yummy snacks and have giggle attacks when you should be sleeping. It can also be called a 'slumber party' or 'pyjama party'.**❞**

❝But what if our new Mate has the kind of parents who just, like, say 'No way' to her having a sleepover?**❞**

Hmm, that's a tough one, Bub, but there are ways around it...

Winning The Parents' permission

There are many ways to get The Parents to let you have a sleepover party. Let's run through the different approaches to "The Wheedle", as we Best Mates like to call it.

Beg: Hands clasped, down on bended knee, whiny voice: "Oh pur-leeeeasssse" etc.

Tantrum: Foot stomping, bedroom door slamming ... and general brat-like behaviour until they "surrender".

Bully/bribe: Said with humphy voice: "If you don't let me, I don't see how I can possibly concentrate on my schoolwork." Similarly: "I promise I'll work double-hard at school."

Nag relentlessly: Like begging, only 24 hours a day: "Go on, go on, go on" etc.

Suck up: "You know I really think you're the best parents a girl could get" etc.

Weep: Silent, dignified dewdrops dabbed gracefully away or great snotty howls – you decide.

Sulk: Dark looks and absolutely zero speech.

The classic: To Dad: "But Mum said I could" and vice versa. Or: "But you promised last year!"

The birthday special: Wailed with real injustice: "But it's MY BIRTHDAY!!!"

Whether you try out these approaches on your mum or dad, or both together, what you are looking for is a crack in their armour – a sign that they might be weakening. Once you spot this – go for it big time!

if i really wnt something i txt mssge mum's moby with ☺ or ☹ faces, depending on if she sez yes or no

If The Wheedle campaign fails you, and you don't have a mobile phone like our spoiled Missy, we Best Mates suggest a formal written letter, like this:

Dear Mr & Mrs _____ (your last name here)

Please let your loving daughter _____ (your name here) have _____ (number of guests here) mates to stay for a sleepover on the night of _____ (date here). If you do we hereby promise that we shall tidy up after ourselves, keep the noise down and turn you into some sort of legend of cool parentdom across the playgrounds of this great country of ours.

Sincerely
(potential sleepover guests and hostess sign here)

❝And if they STILL won't give in, what's a girl to do?**❞**

There's only one desperate option remaining, I'm afraid: the "I'm really a very sensible young lady" approach. This is how it's done: ask your parents to sit down for a few minutes to talk about your proposed sleepover, then show them the following tips for parents. Finally, offer to discuss in a CALM and MATURE way the worries they may still have about your proposed sleepover.

a bit of creeping will get u a long way m8!

Five parental rules for stress-free sleepovers

1 Make sure the girls have lots of energetic activities planned – it keeps them out of trouble and tires them out for bedtime.

2 Provide a few healthy snacks for them to eat with the junk food to prevent sickness and hyperactivity.

3 Establish the rules in a very brief pre-party "chat" – no fighting, crank phone calls, mean tricks, leaving the house or unsupervised cooking – and set a bedtime.

4 Suggest they watch an hour or so of videos before bedtime. They'll soon be nodding off.

5 Avoid embarrassing your beloved daughter, by staying out of the way (except when needed).

So have you persuaded your mum and dad? Hurrah! (If not, turn to the Best Mates' problem solver on page 98, for further advice.) That means you're ready for the next step on the road to sleepover success. Now you can start making plans – things are about to get really exciting!

Molly has a quiet word about M-O-N-E-Y

Call me Mrs Fussypants, but before you get carried away ordering a bucket of the finest cookieslurp-doublefudge-monkeynugget ice cream delivered on matching white ponies for each of your fabulous guests, let's enjoy a sensible moment: how much money can you spend? You don't need a lot of money to make your party fun, but working out a budget will mean you make the most of what you have got.

We want this to be a relaxing, enjoyable day (and night!) and planning ahead of time is the key. A good place to start is by making lots of lovely lists.

The how-to-do-a-sleepover-list list!

1 Write down EVERYTHING you need for your sleepover (people, invites, food, games, videos, DVDs, etc.)

2 Do a satisfying tick as each thing is sorted out...

3 ... or add "**X**" next to worrisome, difficult-to-sort-out things.

4 Write down costs of *everything*, doing scribblings-out and revisions as you go.

5 Get a clipboard if you want to look like a pro.

6 Make sure you've sorted out your "**X**" bits by the morning of the sleepover.

7 Do *not* still be clutching this precious list as your friends arrive (so not cool).

❀ Flower's sleepover list ❀

Theme: Valentine's
Guest list: Molly, Missy, Princess, Bubble and me!
Date: 12 Feb (Held on Saturday so we can make Valentine's cards and give them out at school on Monday)
Start time: 7 pm **Finishing:** 11 am the next morning!

Thing!

Invitations:
Pink card for heart-shaped invites . . . .
Glitter pen . . . .
Stamps . . . .

Room arrangements & decorations:
Sort out where everyone is to sleep plus blankets, pillows etc . . . . . .
Balloons and streamers . . . .

Tidy v messy bedroom!!! . . . .
Chocolate love hearts for Best Mates – to let them know how much I lurve them! . .

Food:
Pizza (including toppings and dough) . . . .
Heart-shaped pan (for pizza) . . . .
Crisp-type snacks, soft drinks and stuff for sundaes . . . .
Doughnuts for breakfast . . . .

Entertainment:
Two soppy love story videos . . . .
Valentine's card-making material (including envelopes,
card, love-heart stickers and stamps) . . . .

Posters and lipstick for kissy-kissy poster game (see page 70) . . . . . .

Miscellaneous:
Make sure best PJs are clean . . . .
Check toothpaste and toilet roll levels! . . . .

> **"** Right, here's my Valentine's sleepover superplan. Don't forget to fill in the cost of things, and doodle down any ideas you have along the way! **"**

Action	Progress ✓ done ✗ to do	Cost
Make cards and send out two weeks b4		
Already got		
Buy from shop		
Mum to do week b4 do		
Dad to dig out leftover ones from New Year's Eve as soon as he "finds time" – Put up on morning of do		
2 days b4		
Leave under each Mate's pillow b4 bedtime – aw!		
Buy ingredients day b4 – Set up kitchen by 5.30 pm		
Dig out from cupboard day b4		
Buy day b4		
Dad to nip out first thing in the morning after sleepover		
Mum renting on the morning of do		
Buy weekend b4 – Lay out equipment on desk in my room on day of sleepover		
Save magazines from last month – Go through three days b4 selecting potential snog victims – Beg Mum for old lippies		
Three days b4		
Day b4		

66 Wow! That's dead impressive, Flower! No wonder we all had such a fab time that night! **99**

Hold your galloping horses, though, Mates! Before you begin devising your superplan, there are some MAJOR decisions you've got to make first. I call them the four Ws, and they are the stars of our next chapter.

The Four Ws: When, What, Where and Who

"Ooh, these sound a bit scary!"

Not at all, Bub. These four lovely little words are our chums, 'cos once you've made the big decisions like ...

when to have your do

where you're going to sleep

what kind of theme you want your evening to have

who to invite

... everything will fall magically into place! Honest!

When to do your "do"

You may be tempted to hold your sleepover on a week night if it's for something special like a birthday. This is OK if it's during school hols, but otherwise it's best to hold it on a Saturday night.

"Erm, why?"

66 Because, dummy, you'll be too pooped from partying all night for school the next day, and on Fridays you'll be too pooped from school to party all night! So it's gotta be a Saturday... And, in my experience, the best sleepovers follow a rough timetable, like this... **99**

Princess's sample sleepover schedule

6 pm	Guests arrive – chat, muck about, get changed into pyjamas
7 pm	Pizza-eating
7.30 pm	Making and munching of gooey ice-cream sundaes
8 pm	Games and karaoke
9.30 pm	Videos and popcorn
11 pm	Tooth-brushing and bed
All night	Giggling, pranks, scary storytelling, etc
10 am	Doughnut breakfast (after mammoth lie-in)
10.30 am	Get dressed
11 am	Watch video we made during karaoke the night before
11.15-12 pm	Guests depart (sob!)

Way to go, Princess, that sounds like the **when** is sorted.
Now we've got to think about **where** your guests are
going to sleep!

wot sleep? i
wanna parteee
all night ☺!!!

❝That's why we always call
your do's 'Missy's nosleepovers',
you mad raver!❞

(Said in sensible author's voice…) Thinking about where
you and your mates are going to sleep will give you a
realistic idea of how many you can invite. But it needn't
be a case of "two in my bed and two on the camp bed"
– use your imagination to make the most of the space
available. You may also want to start thinking about **what**
kind of theme you want your sleepover to have. Come
on, let's see what the Best Mates might do…

Flower's exotic emporium

❝I think I must have been a belly dancer in a previous life 'cos I'd love to spend the night in one of those luxury Bedouin tents! Anyway, this is my cheapo version!**❞**

Theme: Hippy-meets-eastern-desert chic

Good for: small bedrooms

Approx number of guests: four

1 See if your parents will let you clear as much furniture (including your bed) out of your room as possible.

2 Cover the floor with cushions or blankets with sheets spread on top.

3 Ask Mum or Dad to change all the light bulbs in your room to coloured ones – creating a softer light and more intimate feel.

4 Waft sandalwood perfume (or similar spicy scent) around for some, ahem, "exotic smells of the East".

5 Finally, for a truly magical touch, string out Christmas fairy lights around the room. Ta-daa! A cosy wee den fit for Arabian princesses!

Bubble's big yee-haw ★ ☾

❝Camping is great fun – but if cloudy skies and poo-poo parents mean that's a no-no, then use your imagination and take a walk on the Wild-West side with me!❞

Theme: Cowgirls go camping

Good for: bigger bedrooms

Approx number of guests: six

1 Make a night sky by getting a load of thin card (old Christmas cards or cereal boxes will do) and cutting out tons of different-sized stars and moon crescents.

2 Paint your shapes with glow-in-the-dark paint – leaving the first side to dry before flipping each over and doing the second side.

3 Make a hole in the top of each shape either by using a hole punch or, if you don't have one, by placing your shape on a magazine or thick newspaper on top of a stable surface (kitchen worktop, etc) and carefully twisting the point of a pair of scissors to create a small hole. Note the use of the word "carefully" there!

4 Thread a piece of cotton (about 80 cm or so in length) through a shape's hole. With the thread halfway through the hole, hold the two ends together and tie in a knot – so you now have a loop of cotton attached to this shape. Repeat with the rest of the shapes.

5 Now hang them from the ceiling, either with securely fixed drawing pins or Blu-tack.

6 Lay out your guests' sleeping bags in a circle.

7 For a brilliant pretend campfire, get the Christmas fairy lights out and place them in a big heap in the centre of the "circle". Turn out all the lights except your "campfire", and admire the twinkling night sky above!

8 Continue your Wild-West theme by serving nachos, hotdogs and baked beans for munchies ... just watch out for the, ahem, "rumble in the Rockies"!

Missy's movie magic

glam up then veg out – every 1 will luv it!

Theme: Glamorous video-thon
Good for: living rooms
Approx number of guests: eight

1 Hire two or three of the latest video/DVD releases – go for a mix like a funny, a weepy and an action or a thriller (but not, like, freaky-nightmare scary).

2 Paint sheets of newspaper red, then lay them down in a "carpet" leading up to your front door, either fixing it down with masking tape or pebbles from the garden.

3 Decorate the walls of your "cinema" with posters of Hollywood heart-throbs you've saved from old magazines – use Blu-tack to avoid marking the walls.

4 Set up your guests' sleeping positions around the telly so everyone gets a good view.

5 Ask everyone to come dressed as their favourite actress, and as each guest arrives, take a picture of them walking up your red carpet all glammed up. Then you'll have hilarious reminders of your evening!

6 Popcorn is a must!

Those are all great ideas, Mates, but what about NOT having your sleepover inside your house? Mum and Dad sometimes let me and my brother camp out in our caravan parked out the back of our house – it's got a mini TV and fridge and it's brilliant fun. Or you could borrow a big tent and sleep in the garden – a real laugh.

66I once had a sleepover at a museum with five of my friends and my mum – we slept right under a dinosaur skeleton! – and it wasn't expensive at all.**99**

Nice one, Princess. That sounds incredible. If you fancy being adventurous with your sleepover location, try ringing the bigger museums or the local tourist board for inspiration.

WATCH IT, Mate!

* If you're in a caravan, secure it from the inside (but make sure you can get out quickly in an emergency).
   * If you're in a tent in the back garden, consider getting a parent to sleep the night in their own tent a short distance away.
   * If you have access to a mobile, keep it close by so you can phone Mum or Dad quickly in an emergency or if you get scared.
* Need the loo? Make sure you go with someone.

And now onward, Mates, to our final and most important W-word!

Who to invite

So, you've got an idea of your budget, what the theme is going to be and how many guests you can accommodate. The big decision that now faces you is which of your trazillions of friends are you gonna invite and who are you going to leave out? Princess, you know a thing or two about "etiquette" (posh word for "rules"). Any thoughts?

Princess's pointers on the perilous pitfalls of the party guestlist

1. Only invite people you know are going to get on – bickering is so not fun.

2. Invite people you want to invite, not people that you feel you have to invite ('cos so-and-so invited you to theirs). Remember it's YOUR party.

3. Bear in mind that if you invite too many people, they may split off into smaller groups which could cause tension. Also, large numbers mean you have to play the hostess and may not be able to spend as much time relaxing and enjoying yourself - not good.

4. Instead of handing out your invites in school and risk upsetting those not invited, either post them or send an email invite.

5. If you find out a friend who hasn't been invited is feeling left out, be honest and explain that you're only allowed limited numbers; then ask her to do something else with you, like going to the cinema or shopping.

6. Send out your invites well in advance so people have time to reply and also so they don't get booked up.

Designing your invites

The thing with any invite is that it must contain essential information about where and when, etc.

doh! how obvious!????

Ahem, I am thinking here about a certain person's birthday bash when that person forgot to put THE DATE of her do on the invite. Ring any ringtones, Nora?

ok u got me ... and dont call me that! anyway since then ive txt some notes, which u r welcome 2 share with r m8

missy's no-mistakes invite info checklist

yr name ☺ yr address ☺ yr phone number – so panicky parents have contact number ☺ date, start time & finish time – so panicky parents know when 2 pick up beloved daughter ☺ rsvp deadline – so u know how many guests u got coming & if someone can't come 2 give u time to invite someone else ☺ list of items u want yr guests 2 bring eg: sleeping bag ☺ pillow ☺ fanciest pjs/nightie ☺ other fancy-dress costume in keeping with yr theme if ur having 1 ☺ toothbrush ☺ torch ☺ vids, dvds, cds ☺ make-up, nail varnish, body glitter, wigs(!) & any other stuff 4 makeovers

Awesome texting there, Missy. That's the invite contents sorted, but what about how the invitation looks? Ladies and, erm, ladies, I give you:

How to make the best sleepover invites in the world ... ever!

The mini-pillow invite

You will need:

★ Plain white card (10 cm x 8 cm for each invite)
★ Cotton material – like a cut-up old pillowcase (25 cm x 18 cm for each invite) ★ Cotton wool ★ Glue

What you do:

1 Place the material pattern-side down (if it has a pattern!), fold over a 2-cm hem down one of the longer edges and glue down.

2 Turn your material over (so pattern is face-up) and put a thin strip of glue along the edges of the other three sides.

3 Fold the material in half so that the two shorter ends meet and press the glued edges together.

4 Wait for glue to dry, then turn your "pillowcase" inside out. If the material is patterned, this will now be on the outside.

5 Having written your invite on the card (use glitter pens and gold stars to jazz them up), stuff this into the pillowcase (trimming card edges if necessary) and plump up your dinky pillow with the cotton wool.

66Aw, this sounds sooo cute!**99**

66Nah! Us sophisticated
types think this next one is
the business.**99**

The jet-set invite

The idea is that your invite will look like one of those neat
travel packs you get on long air flights.

You will need:

★ Miniature travel-size toothpaste tubes and brushes
★ Plastic sandwich bags – the ones with the zip-lock tops
★ Plain card (about 12 cm x 8 cm for each invite)

What you do:

1 Cut your card into a luggage-tag shape by snipping off two of the corners at one end, and drawing a "hole" at that end.

2 Write out your invite on the tag in the style of a luggage label.

Bubble, you're always going abroad with your folks. Perhaps you can show our Mate what you'd put if you were doing a jet-set invite?

❝No problem! OK, here's my effort:❞

To: **Ms Molly White**

(First–class passenger – make way!!!)

From: Bubble of 3 Cherry Tree Crescent, Dullsville, Spamshire

(In the Kingdom of Bubbleonia)

Via: **Sleepover at my place**

(Please bring own sleeping bag & pillow)

Arrival: **6 pm, Saturday 17 July**

Depart: **11 am, Sunday 18 July**

International enquiry no: 00 (44) 1 234 56 7890

Please confirm your seat (or bed!) by: 5 July

New York, Paris, Bubbleonia!

Excellent stuff, Bubs! Now this is what you need to finish off.

3 Pop your toothpaste into the bag, along with the invite, and "zip" shut.
4 (optional) If you're putting your jet-set invite into an outer envelope, then decorate it with travel-themed graffiti, for example, "I'm collecting airhead miles!", "Taking it easy on the Zambezi", "Tickety-boo in Timbuktu", etc.

Of course, you can have fun creating your own wacky invite...

★ ★ ★ ★ ★ ★ ★ ★ ★ ★ ★ ★ ★ ★ ★ ★

The all-purpose invite
You will need:
Card ★ Envelopes ★ Paint ★ Glue ★ Glitter ★ Plastic gemstones ★ Photos of your guests ★ Anything else you can think of!

What you do:
1 If you're having a theme for your sleepover, try to create a design based on that. For example, a star-shaped invite is good for a Hollywood theme.

2 Personalize each guest's invite by cutting out their face from a photo (if you haven't got a photo, sneakily ask their mums for one) and fix it on to a pic of a celeb's body cut from a magazine. If you're feeling more artistic, you could draw them with angel wings and a halo or devil horns and a tail – or whatever else inspires you!

3 Make your invite a mad, multi-coloured thing of glistening beauty by gluing on masses of glitter, plastic gems, and anything else pretty and sparkly you've got.

So, dear Mate, once you've sorted (or at least vaguely thought about!) when to hold your do, where it's going to take place, what the vibe's going to be and who's coming, you can start to think about what we in the party-planning business call the, ahem, "cuisine".

"Yipeee! We're talking grub – my very favourite subject!"

34

Scrummy Sleepover Scoff

"Ooh, I've got a recipe for pizza that our Mate must make!**"**

nofink compares
2 missy's float-my-
boat coke

"I tell you, the way to impress your guests is with chic nibbles like dips and crudités.**"**

crudy wot?!

"Vegetable sticks."

"What's wrong with getting a pizza delivery?"

"I'm just thinking healthy, that's all!"

OK, Mates, cool it! Before we start squabbling about what slurpacious suggestions to offer our Mate, we've one problem left to deal with – the kitchen.

wot's wrong with the kitchen?

In a word: Mum!

Mums and kitchens

The thing with mums (and the odd dad) is that they get really nervous at the thought of you and a few girl pals entering their kitchen. Their top three worries are that you will:

a) cut off your fingers;

b) burn the house down;

c) and – oh, the pain they suffer! – make a "mess".

So, what is a girl to do?

❝Ooh, I've got the answer to this one! I had a sleepover a couple of years ago and felt sure that me and the Mates were old enough to be left to make our own food. This is the conversation I had with my mum a few days before my sleepover…❞

Princess's step-by-step guide to getting your mum out of the kitchen and you in!

The scenario:

Princess: "Mum, I thought for my sleepover, we'd do dips for starters, jacket potatoes with various fillings, then a huge gooey sundae for afters."

Mrs Moxbury: "Ooh, lovely dear. I'll be happy to do it."

"Here's how I solved the problem:**"**

1 Make your mum feel needed

Princess: "Well, it'd be great if you could help out with the shopping, but I thought me and the Mates would cook, as that's half the fun. Although I'd really, really appreciate it if you could be on hand, just in case; like, maybe relaxing in the living room."

2 The bribe

Princess: "Oh look, talking of which, I bought you that new magazine you were after. You could read that, have a cup of tea and put your feet up for a change."

Mrs M: "But, but, but..."

3 The killer move

Princess: "Oh, and I've typed up a list of kitchen safety rules and conditions of use for your approval, which all the Mates have read and signed."

4 Put your mum into a state of shock

Mrs M: (shocked and stunned, taking list): "Erm, I suppose so, dear. Thank you."

Princess's code of safety for kitchen use and accompanying parent-pleasing promises

Dear parents of _____ (your name here)
we, the undersigned, hereby promise to:

1. Be very cautious when using sharp knives – cutting everything slowly and carefully.
2. Be very careful when handling hot stuff – always using oven gloves and moving slowly and carefully.
3. Call you if we have any difficulties.
4. Turn off appliances when not in use.
5. Not goof about too much.
6. Tidy up as we go along.
7. Wash our hands.
8. Be very grateful that our dear friend _____ (your name here) has such an excellent and indeed very groovy parent.

Signed _____

(you all sign here)

"Right, now you've got your mum out of the way, let's talk scoff!**"**

Calm down, Bubs, we're going to talk food right now!

Now that you've wheedled your way into the kitchen you'll be needing the Best Mates' recipes and tips for the ultimate sleepover cuisine for you to consider serving at your do. Drool on, Mate!

Hearty and wholesome: first courses

"Urrgh! Sounds like stuff my gran would make me eat!**"**

Don't worry, Bubs, these are the yummy savouries that will prepare our Mate's tummy for the icky-goo that follows later! Actually, the first thing on the menu is pizza, and since you're the pizza queen, Bubs, I nominate you to be the first one to share your know-how with our Mate.

Bubble's brilliant guide to pizza-eating

"Pick up phone. Dial pizza man. Order. Wait. Pay delivery person. Eat pizza."

"Ha ha! Only joking! Ordering in pizza is cool, but it's expensive and nowhere near as much fun as making your own. So come on, Mate, let's bake!"

Get your dough

"There are two options here, buy ready-made pizza bases from the supermarket or, for a really impressive (and scrummier and super-cheap) option, make your own dough before your guests arrive. Don't worry, it's easy-peasy!"

The Best Mates' EZ pizza dough
For one biggy pizza or four diddlers you will need:
★ One 7 g packet of dry yeast ★ 225 ml warm water
★ One 5 ml spoon (a teaspoon) sugar ★ One 5 ml spoon
(a teaspoon) salt ★ Two 15 ml spoons (two tablespoons)
olive oil ★ 330 g plain flour or strong white flour

What you do:

1 Preheat the oven to 220° C (gas mark 7).

2 Dissolve the yeast in the water.

3 In a separate bowl, mix all the other ingredients, then bung in the yeast mixture to bind it together.

4 On a floury surface, knead the dough together by pushing and pulling it with clenched fists for five minutes. (It helps to think of a stinky maths teacher at this point.)

5 Form the dough into a large ball. Rub a small amount of olive oil round a clean bowl, then pop the dough into this bowl, covering it with a clean tea towel. Leave the bowl somewhere warm for about 45 minutes. The yeast will make the dough "rise" and become spongy.

6 Grease a baking tray, then, with floured paws, roll dough out into a pizza shape, about 0.5–1 cm thick.

7 When your mates arrive, stack on desired toppings (see over the page).

8 Bake for 20–25 minutes. Scrum-diddly-umcious!

❝Hey, Bubble, can I tell our Mate about the most delish veggie topping in the world, ever? You know, the 'Herbal Burble' I invented at our last pizza fest?!❞

66 Ooh, yeah. That's a good un! 99

Flower's herbal burble pizza

66 I love this 'cos it's all light and creamy and the herbs give it a really subtle, delicious flavour. 99

You will need:

★ Small tub ricotta cheese (or other soft cream cheese)
★ One 15 ml spoon (tablespoon) olive oil ★ A few torn-up basil leaves or sprinkle of dried basil (about half a teaspoon) ★ Sprinkle of oregano (like, just a quarter of a teaspoon) ★ One clove garlic, chopped (optional) ★ One tomato, sliced ★ Big handful of grated cheese (mozzarella or cheddar)

What you do:

1 Mix together chopped garlic, ricotta, oil and basil and spread over pizza base.

2 Put on tomato, sprinkle on oregano and cover with grated cheese.

* * * * * * * * * * * * * * * * * *

Slap it on mama-mia!

❝This one makes everyone happy! Each person gets their own individual pizza base and then shoves on whatever they want from the following ingredients (deep breath):**❞**

Meats: ham, pepperoni, crispy bacon, cooked and chopped chicken, cooked meatballs, fried mince.

Fish: tuna, prawns, seafood mix, crab sticks, anchovies.

❝Anchovies! Errrgh! How totally gross!**❞**

Veggies: tomato, peppers, mushroom, sweetcorn, onion, spring onion, artichoke (v posh!), cooked spinach.

Cheese: mozzarella (can't be beat for stringiness), cheddar, parmesan (smells like sick, but tastes gorge), edam, blue cheese... In fact, ALL cheeses are acceptable. Hurrah!

Other stuff: tomato purée (or any other thick tomato sauce), pesto sauce, sprinkles of dried oregano or basil, black pepper, olives, garlic, chillies (but go easy there!), BBQ sauce (very yummy with chicken!), capers, pineapple, egg (either boiled and chopped or plopped raw in the centre before entering the oven – make sure it's cooked through before you eat it, though!).

❝Get each of your guests to do a 'pizza portrait' of someone else. The results are mad! Here's one I did of Princess:❞

Molly's pizza Princess portrait

1 For her pale complexion, I used ricotta cheese covered in grated mozzarella.

2 For her big eyes, I got two mushrooms, removed the stalks, and put them cap-side down.

3 Her blubbery lips. Sorry, I meant, lovely. Her lovely lips were made using slices of red pepper.

4 Two juicy slices of tomato became her gorgeous cheeks.

5 Her nose was made from a triangular wedge of ham.

6 Finally, her beautiful strawberry-blonde hair was recreated with strips of cheddar smeared lightly with tomato puree.

❝Hmm, thanks for that, I think. Anyway, now we've done pizza, I want to tell you about those crudités and dips.❞

❝Boo! 'Healthy' food. Bore-ring!❞

❝Ooh, you cheeky madam! I seem to remember you scoffing your share at my last sleepover. In case anyone else thinks like Bubble, I guarantee they are irresistibly munchy AND they don't make you feel sick! I've dedicated these two recipes to their greatest fans.**❞**

★ ★ ★ ★ ★ ★ ★ ★ ★ ★ ★ ★ ★ ★ ★ ★ ★ ★ ★

Hippy dippy humous for Flower

For four people you will need:

★ One can chickpeas ★ One garlic clove, finely chopped ★ Two 15 ml spoons (two tablespoons) tahini paste (made from sesame seeds and available in most supermarkets, but you could replace it with a couple of spoons of peanut butter) ★ One lemon ★ Two 15 ml spoons (two tablespoons) olive oil ★ Two 15 ml spoons (two tablespoons) water

What you do:

1 Drain chickpeas and (after telling Mum or Dad what you're up to) whirl them in a blender with juice from the lemon, chopped garlic and tahini paste or peanut butter. If you haven't got a blender, place ingredients in

48

a large bowl and mash up using a potato masher or fork (take it in turns when your arm aches!).

2 Drizzle in the oil and water until your humous reaches a "dippy" consistency.

* * * * * * * * * * * * * * * * *

Gorge guacamole for Golly Ms Molly

❝ Ta, love! Is there a finer dip known to girlkind? I think not! **❞**

For four people you will need:
★ One large ripe avocado (has to be ripe!) ★ Two spring onions, chopped ★ One garlic clove, finely chopped ★ One tomato (or a couple of scoops from a tin of chopped tomatoes. ★ One lime or half a lemon ★ Dash of chilli sauce (optional)

What you do:
1 Plop tomato into cup of boiling water (careful, now!).
2 Peel and roughly chop avocado and place in a bowl, pour over squeezed juice from lime or lemon (stops

avocado going yucky grey colour), add onions and garlic. Mush together using a potato masher or the back of a fork.

3 Take tomato from cup and remove skin – give it a gentle squeeze and it should peel off easily. Chop skinned tomato into smallish chunks, and stir into guacamole with a dash of the chilli sauce.

What a delicious couple of dips, Princess. One question, though – what should we dip? Time for a vote, methinks!

The Best Mates' top five dunkers

For the immersing in and retrieving of dip, we hereby declare the winners as follows:

1 Veggie sticks (sliced peppers, carrots, celery, cucumber)

2 Toasted pitta bread cut into wedges

3 Tortilla chips

4 Bread sticks

5 Fingers (gross, but true!)

WATCH IT, Mate!

Keep those hands clean – especially when cooking or putting fingers into dips – yeurrrgh!

And finally, here comes the...

Best dag nabbit sandwich known to girlkind!!!

best wot?

Well, I could have said quesadilla (pronounced *case-ah-dee-ah*) but you wouldn't have known what I was talking about.

They're actually a kind of Mexican cheese sandwich. Bubble and I had them at that Tex-Mex place in town and we agreed they were the, ahem, best dag nabbit (cowboy for extremely good) sandwich, like, ever and simply had to be sampled at our next sleepover. The cute waiter told us they were dead easy to make and gave us this recipe:

Cute waiter's quesadilla recipe
To make one sandwich (serves two) you need:
★ Two flour tortilla breads ★ Two handfuls grated cheese
★ Blob of butter

What you do:

1 Heat butter in large frying pan and swish around.

2 Put one tortilla on a plate and spread cheese over bread to the edges.

3 Place second tortilla on top.

4 Carefully transfer your sandwich to the pan (be careful it doesn't fall apart by sliding a spatula underneath and using your spare hand to keep the top on).

5 Cook for a couple of minutes on each side (you want the cheese to be melted and the bread lightly browned). Cut into four delicious pieces.

And if that's not the best sandwich in the West, I'll eat my ten-gallon hat!

"You can also add loads of other things to the cheese – like onions, ham, tomatoes, sandwich pickle, yee-haw!**"**

Something to slurp: beverages and such

From American-style ice-cream-float sodas to pudding-in-a-glass cocktails ... what would a sleepover be without someone somewhere making a pukey concoction in a glass? These are the BMs' faves. (Big straws are a must for top slurrrpability!)

Princess's pina colada

You will need:

★ 60 ml coconut milk ★ Small can pineapple chunks ★ Four ice cubes' worth of crushed ice (put in placcy bag and bash with rolling pin) ★ Spray cream and cherry (optional)

What you do:

Whisk everything together in a blender. Or, if you haven't got a blender, use a can of crushed pineapple or 150 ml of pineapple juice (although it won't be quite as slushy!). Top with spray cream and a cherry, if you've got them.

"Looks and tastes divine, darling!"

do u remember when we made these and yr mum gave us those cocktail umbrellas? we looked so cool, man!

★ ★ ★ ★ ★ ★ ★ ★ ★ ★ ★ ★ ★ ★ ★ ★ ★ ★ ★ ★

Flower's healing smoothie

You will need:

★ One frozen banana (or fresh if you haven't got a blender) ★ Two handfuls of soft fresh fruit (strawberries, melon, kiwi, etc) ★ 170 ml fruit juice (any kind)

What you do:

Give it all a whirl in the blender, pour, sip and think peaceful thoughts! (Those of you without blenders will have to mash the fruit using a potato masher, adding the juice slowly as you go.)

66 After sports day last year, I felt exhausted, but after Flower made me one of these smoothies I felt like I could run a marathon! **99**

* * * * * * * * * * * * * * * * *

Missy's float-my-boat coke

u need: cola ☺ vanilla ice cream

wot u do: half fill tall glass with cola, top with 2 scoops of ice cream

66 A friend of mine does this with cream soda and strawberry ice cream – it's so dreamy. Sickly, but dreamy. **99**

66 What's next? Personally, I think our Mate will need lashings of sweet stuff at her sleepover. Whaddya think, Molly?! **99**

You've got it, Bubble.

* * * * * * * * * * * * * * * * *

Sweet gooey glory: pudding!

Me and the Best Mates agree that when it comes to sleepover puddings you just gotta do the ultimate sundae experience, otherwise known as (cue thriller-movie-style sound effect) dun dun dun…

The Abominable Sundae!!

The Abominable is a mix of four key sundae ingredients. You need at least one from each of the following categories but you can use as many as you like.

1 Frozen stuff: ice cream, frozen yoghurt or sorbet.

2 Gooey oozy pourers: chocolate, fudge, raspberry or strawberry sauce, maple syrup and (Best Mates' fave) melted chocolate bars (see box).

3 Smoosh-ins: broken-up biscuits, crushed chocolate bars, squishy fruit, cereals and sweets.

4 Fancy finishes: drinking-chocolate powder (sprinkled), glacé cherries, flaked chocolate sticks, sprinkles (like hundreds and thousands, chopped nuts, etc).

The messy business of melting chocolate bars

66 OK, so melting perfectly good choc bars is the kinda thing only the most twisted of adolescent chocoholics will attempt. But I promise you, Mate, once you've mastered the divine art, there's not a dish in the land that can't be improved with a yummy dollop of choccie gloop! **99**

To melt chocolate:

1 Heat a saucepan half filled with water until the water bubbles a bit.

2 Place a ceramic or glass bowl, which is a bit larger than the saucepan, on top of the pan. The bowl should touch the water but not the bottom of the pan.

3 Break up chocolate into pieces and put into bowl.

4 Turn heat down low and stir chocolate occasionally as it melts.

Note: If your bar is solid chocolate it will take around three to four minutes to melt. However, if your chosen bar contains things other than chocolate – toffee, caramel, nuts, etc – it will take around five to eight minutes to melt. Overheating causes choc to go all stiff and weird – if this happens, add a bit of cream or vegetable oil and carry on melting the chocolate until it's smooth.

To do The Abominable

1 Get the biggest bowl you can find in the house and lay out whatever you've got of the four key ingredients. All gather round the sacred bowl.

2 Pile in scoops of as many kinds of frozen stuff as you've got to form a base.

3 Smother with chosen gooey oozy pourer.

4 In a mad frenzy, everyone add their fave smoosh-ins at once – then squidge into the ice cream using the back of your spoon (the "smooshing" bit).

5 Garnish with as much whipped cream and fancy finishes as possible.

6 Grab spoon, crowd round bowl and let the scoffing begin!

66 Urgh, all that talk of gooey choc has made me feel sick. **99**

Oh no, not again! Poor Flower, she always comes over all queasy even after the weensiest bit of scrummy sleepover scoff. So, let's slip on our sensible pants for a moment, and think about what we should do in the event of one of you feeling a bit dodgy.

Molly has a quiet word about feeling queasy

* Get some air – either take a stroll in the garden or sit by an open window.
* Sip some water.
* Focus on something else – try watching a video or chat quietly.
* Don't panic if you do throw up – if it's the result of eating too much, you'll usually begin to feel better within an hour. You should, however, call for a parent's help if this happens.

66 Thanks, Molly. Actually, I am feeling a bit better now. Let's carry on! **99**

& now 4 my fave kinda food – quick fix stuff 4 girls who wanna get on with tha party! m8, we give u...

No fuss movie munchies and all-night snack attacks

Tex-Mex popcorn

You will need:

★ Big bowl of freshly popped popcorn (equal to about 150 g of pre-popped corn) ★ One 15 ml spoon (one tablespoon) of taco seasoning ★ 60 g butter ★ 85 g grated cheddar cheese

"Do you remember that time we put chopped jalapeño chillies in, not realizing how hot they were? We had to drink cold milk for about three hours afterwards!**"**

and then my brother thought it was leftovers & finished half the bowl b4 the chillie hit! then boy did it hit!

What you do:

1 Put popcorn in large bowl.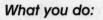

2 Melt the butter by whacking in the microwave for 15–30 seconds on high, or heating it in a small pan on the cooker.

3 Stir in the seasoning and mix in with the popcorn and cheese.

★ ★ ★ ★ ★ ★ ★ ★ ★ ★ ★ ★ ★ ★ ★ ★ ★

Caramel popcorn

66 Serve as an 'afters' to the Tex-Mex: a winning double snack! **99**

You will need:

★ Big bowl of freshly popped popcorn (equal to about 150 g of pre-popped corn) ★ 110 g butter (leave it out of the fridge, so it's not rock hard) ★ 110 g dark brown sugar

What you do:

1 Squash butter with wooden spoon, then add the brown sugar and beat until the sugar is combined and the mixture is light and creamy.

2 Toss popcorn with butter mixture in a large roasting tin and put the lot in hot, preheated oven (around 190° C/ gas mark 5) for about eight minutes or until crispy.

★ ★ ★ ★ ★ ★ ★ ★ ★ ★ ★ ★ ★ ★ ★ ★ ★ ★

❝I love this next one 'cos it's so much classier than your typical junky snack!**❞**

❝Said like a true princess! And she's right – even I feel dead sophisticated scoffing these.**❞**

Choco-dipped strawberries
You will need:
★ Punnet of strawberries (leave the stems on) ★ Two medium-sized chocolate bars (white, plain or milk!) ★ 60 g butter

What you do:
1 Wash and dry strawbs.
2 Melt chocolate (see page 57) with the butter, giving it a good stir.

3 Hold strawberry by stem and dip it into the chocolate. Lift out with a twist and place it on a plate lined with greaseproof paper. Repeat with the rest.

4 Pop them in the fridge until chocolate sets (usually about an hour).

 Best Mates **TOP TIP** — If you can't be bothered to wait for the chocolate to set, use the warm chocolate as a dip, with everyone doing their own dunking (you gotta be quick before it sets – but mind it's not too hot before popping it into your chops).

Of course, dear Mate, you'll probably want to offer some crisp-style packet snacks at your do. But there are so many different kinds, and different brands, how on earth is a girl meant to decide which ones to spend her hard-wheedled cash on?! Avoid a crisp crisis with our simple but genius snack-o-meter.

Before your sleepover, ask each of your guests what their favourite snacks are in order of preference. Award each snack the following points:

No 1 favourite snack = 5 points ★ No 2 snack = 4 points ★ No 3 snack = 3 points ★ No 4 snack = 2 points ★ No 5 snack = 1 point.

Count up each snack's score and work out the top five. Then fill in the snack-o-meter below. You will then know which snacks to buy for your crew! Clever, huh? (Alternatively, just do it on the night of your sleepover – having bought a good selection beforehand – it's funny how passionate a girl can get over a crisp vote!)

The Best Mates' packet snack-o-meter

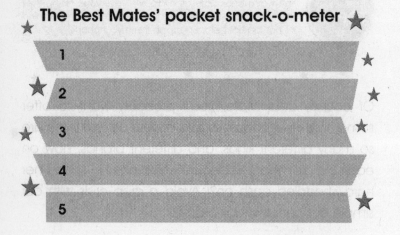

1

2

3

4

5

OK, BMs. What are your favourites?

crisps-in-a-tube – the sour cream and chive ones. they r funky!

66Garlicky tortilla chips –
'cos they remind me of
when I went to Spain.**99**

66Smoky BBQ kettle
chips – they're simply
delectable, darling.**99**

66Pistachio nuts – it's fun
to crack them open, they're
delicious and they're good
for you!**99**

I can't believe none of you mentioned cheese puffs, surely the most heavenly of all the world's glorious snacks? No? Just me, is it? Oh, well, moving on swiftly...

Sending your guests off with a breakfast banquet fit for a queen

Ha! Not really! Truth is, you'll probably be too tired from the night before to bother cooking an actual banquet! Any thoughts, Mates?

66 The easiest thing to do is to supply a few well chosen items and allow your ravenous chums to grab what they want. Like this...**99**

Princess's (and Bubble's) essential top ten breakfast items

1 Orange juice

2 Doughnuts

3 Pop-up waffles...

4 ...and maple syrup to go with

5 Toasted bagels...

6 ...and cream cheese to go with

7 Chocolate croissants

8 Greek-style yoghurt

9 Bananas

10 Leftover pizza (pig-like behaviour, but Bubble insisted I included it)

"Ain't nothing tastier than last night's pizza for breakfast!"

Mmm! Thank you, Princess and, erm, Bubble.

So, Mate, that's our top tuck tips (try saying that with a mouthful of sticky popcorn!) sorted. You're probably thinking that a sleepover with such superior scoffing can get no better – but that's because you haven't yet read about our splendiferous schemes for entertaining your bedazzled guests. Read on, and find out how to get your sleepover really jumping.

Stuff to Do

> **"**All the best sleepovers have a scary storytelling session.**"**

> **"**I hate that bit! My favourite thing is makeovers – I still cry laughing thinking about when we turned Molly into Fangy, the evil zombie Teletubby, last Halloween!**"**

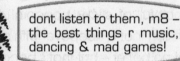

dont listen to them, m8 – the best things r music, dancing & mad games!

OK, BMs, TURN THE VOLUME DOWN! I need to have a quiet word with our new Mate.

Molly has a quiet word about doing stuff

Now, dear Mate, what the BMs are trying to say (in their confused and shouty way) is that there are loads of different activities you can do to keep your lovely guests entertained. And while you probably won't manage them all, you need to decide before your party begins what stuff you'd like to do and then make the necessary pre-party preparations. Otherwise, you might decide you want to do something and find you can't because you haven't got the right equipment (eg, for karaoke) – and then squabbles break out between your guests about what they want to do and your sleepover quickly becomes a sulkover. Yikes indeed!

The five best girly games for sleepovers (in reverse order)

5 The mummy game
Object of the game:
To be the fastest team to turn a player into a mummy (not the type that sits in an armchair and worries, but the spooky kind from Egypt).

You will need:
★ Four rolls of toilet paper

What you do:
1 Split into two teams. Each team is armed with two new toilet rolls.

2 Nominate a mummy.

3 The first team to completely wrap their mummy wins!

Pre-party prep: Make sure you've got stacks of loo roll!

66 Everyone always wants me to be the mummy 'cos I'm short, so I don't take up much loo roll! Still, at least I'm usually on the winning team! 99

Best Mates
TOP TIP

Play some lively music during the game – it will add to the madness! Also, be sure to take a picture of each team posing with their finished mummy.

★

4 ★ **The kissy-kissy poster game**
★ ★
Object of the game:

To be the girl who plants a smacker nearest to the hot celeb's luscious lips.

You will need:

★ Poster of boy-hunk ★ Blu-tack ★ Horrendous-coloured lipstick

What you do:

1 Put up a poster of your fave male celebrity on the wall.

2 Before each girl's turn, thickly paint her lips with the brightest lipstick you've got.

3 Blindfold her and spin her around ten times.

4 Point her in the direction of poster and get her to snog away!

5 The girl whose lips are closest to the hunk's mouth gets to keep the lippy-covered poster as her prize.

Pre-party prep: Go through your old mags to get posters and beg Mum for old lippy.

WATCH IT, Mate!

If the snogger is about to plant a lurid pink lip-print on The Parents' fancy floral wallpaper, appoint a steerer to guide her clear, or all yell wildly in unison to put her back on course. Alternatively, carefully tack up a large expanse of newspaper under the poster to protect the wall.

Boogie boogie dooo dance competition!

3

Object of the game:

Each team battles for the Boogie Cup by making up a brilliant dance routine.

You will need:

★ Stereo or ghetto blaster ★ A couple of dance music CDs ★ Wacky outfits (optional) ★ Any other mad props you might want to use in your dance ★ The Boogie Cup (it's great to have a proper prize to give out – but it needn't be expensive; an el cheapo mug or mock-crystal glass would be really funny)

What you do:

1 Divide into teams (pairs are good).

2 Give each team 20 minutes to come up with their dance routine.

3 If everyone is going to dance to the same track, keep replaying it as everyone is rehearsing. If each team wants different tracks, take it in turns to rehearse while the others get on with something else.

4 The hostess should decide who the winners are.

Pre-party prep: Sort out some music and buy prize (optional). Warn your guests about the competition on their invites, asking them to come with an "appropriate" outfit.

Best Mates TOP TIP

Video each team's efforts (if your family doesn't have a camcorder, try to borrow one for the evening – it'll be worth it!) and watch the results in the morning as your breakfast entertainment.

" Missy is a brilliant dancer and nearly always wins. Why not share a few tips with our Mate, Missy? **"**

u got it!

Missy's dance class
(As translated into normal speak by your Author for ease of reading!)

Keep it low'n'funky!

If you want to get that urban, hip-hop look keep your hips way low and your knees bent slightly. It's all in da attitood, girlfriend!

Perfect the body ripple!

You know the move – the one they do in all the pop videos where it looks as though an invisible force is passing through the dancer's body? It looks so professional and yet it's sooo simple to do.

1 Stand with your feet and knees together – with your body relaxed, almost slumped.

2 Flex your knees slightly, bend forward at the waist and tuck your head down so your chin is touching your chest.

3 Push your knees forward followed by your hips. (As you do this your upper body will start to become upright again – still keep your chin tucked in.)

4 Allow your top half to tilt backwards slightly but stay balanced as you carry on pushing your hips forward.

5 Finish by releasing your chin as your head flicks backwards. You are now perfectly upright.

6 Keep practising, take it slowly and think of yourself as a big gloopy milkshake – you'll soon master it!

Co-ordinate, Mate

If there are two of you, think of how you're standing in relation to one another – try back to back or face to face and keep your moves the same – it'll look really neat (try co-ordinating a ripple!). Don't attempt anything too complicated, just try repeating a series of moves, maybe using more of your space each time.

Camp it up! (Molly *always* does this one!)

Express the lyrics of the song with some dramatic "interpretations". For example, if it's a mushy lurve song stick your hand under your top and push the material forward in time to the music so it looks as though your heart is beating. Try using some mad props – grab those balloons and experiment!

Bonkers rock-out (Bubble *always* does this one!)

Can't dance? Won't dance? Simple. Jump up and down as madly as you can, shaking your head back and forth and roaring like a hungry dinosaur. Spectators will simply be stunned by the, ahem, *energy* of your performance.

WATCH IT, Mate!

Jumping up and down after quaffing huge quantities of sleepover scoff will probably have spectators gawping at your "technicolour yawn" (slang for being sick!) rather than your "technical brilliance". Our advice? Let your food go down before you *get* down, sister!

2 Karaoke Queen

Object of the game:

To be the sweetly crooning girl beating her dog-yodelling pals to the Karaoke Queen Crown.

You will need:

★ Basic karaoke machine or karaoke CD and lyric sheets ★ Fancy dress (optional) ★ Plastic tiara for the winning queen (optional!)

What you do:

1 Each girl belts out a song of her choice following the lyric sheet – and trying not to lose her place – as the instrumental track blasts along.

2 Each Mate votes for their favourite act (not themselves). In the event of a tie, the hostess casts the deciding vote!

3 Don't forget to video everything – including the crowning "ceremony"!

Pre-party prep: Sort out a karaoke machine. Borrow one if you can, or rent one locally, or – if you're feeling flash – buy one. If that's beyond your limited cash funds, karaoke CDs, tapes, DVDs and videos come complete with lyric sheets and don't cost too much. Buy cheap prize (optional).

Hang on, the Mates' reigning Karaoke Queen would like a word...

Princess's perfect sleepover theme

I love karaoke. (Did I mention I was rather good? Tra la la la la! See?!) Anyway, for my last birthday sleepover I had a disco and karaoke theme. Let me tell you what I did...

1 I converted the dining room into my dancehall-and-sleep room by clearing out the table and chairs.

2 I strung up loads of Christmas tinsel and gold and silver balloons.

3 I made my own glitter ball by hanging a large beach ball covered in tin foil from the centre of the ceiling. Then I got two angle-poise lamps – one with a red bulb and one with a blue bulb – and put them in opposite corners of the room, shining them up at the ball.

4 For the karaoke contest, Mum and Dad borrowed some plastic fruit crates and lined them up against one wall to make a "stage".

5 Then, for a laugh, I got a huge bit of thick, white board, painted an almost life-size picture of a stunning rock chick's curvaceous body, cut out a hole for the head and put it up on stage. Everyone had a go at sticking their face through the hole and having their picture taken! The results were hilarious!

And what a brilliant evening that was, Princess!

OK! And now the moment we've all been waiting for. Mate, I give you...

★ The number one sleepover game of all time: Truth or Dare!!!

Object of the game:

To get your friends to confess hilarious secrets or to make them look very silly indeed.

What you do:

1 Sit in a circle and take it in turns to pick a Truth or a Dare.

2 A Truth means you have to answer a question honestly.

3 A Dare means performing a daft stunt.

Rules:

Don't be mean! This is meant to be a fun game, so don't try to deliberately upset someone or make them perform a stunt that could harm them.

Everyone should agree that what is said is to be treated as top secret and NOT to be repeated as gossip at school.

Pre-party prep: It will help the game run smoothly if you write out "Truths" and "Dares" on slips of paper and put them in two hats (or whatever!) first; it will also make the game much fairer.

The BMs' sample Truths or Dares to get you started

★ TRUTHS

★ When was the last time you picked your nose?

★ What is the meanest thing you've ever said about someone?

★ Who is your most embarrassing relative and why?

★ Describe the last fight you had.

★ If you had to get married tomorrow, who would you marry (NO celebrities!)?

★ Tell us a secret about your sister or brother.

★ If you could change one thing about the way you look what would it be and why?

★ What is the most disgusting thing you've ever done?

★ Pick a word beginning with W to describe yourself.

★ What is the naffest present you've ever been given?

★ Have you ever kissed – or even thought about kissing – a boy? Who? If not, who would you kiss if you HAD to?

★ When was the last time you lied? Who to and why?

★ Which celebrity is the person sitting on your left most like?

★ Tell us a secret.

★ Tell us about something you regret doing.

★ DARES

★ Put your finger up your nose and leave it there for three minutes. Giggling forfeits another minute.

★ Sniff the person on your right's toes. Describe the smell.

★ Sing a song all the way through.

★ Find a teddy bear and have a pretend argument with him/her for one minute.

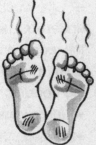

★ Do an impression of the hostess's mum or dad.

★ In a French accent tell the person on your left that you love them and wish to make them your wife.

★ Do a song and dance impression of a current pop act.

★ Find the brightest lipstick you can and – shutting your eyes – give yourself rosy cheeks and pouty lips.

★ Open the window and shout (or whisper loudly if it's late): "____ (your name) is the most beautiful girl in all the world!"

★ Put a pair of knickers on your head and leave them there for three minutes. Giggling forfeits another minute.

★ Using a sock for a nose, pretend you are an elephant by crawling all around the room, swishing your "trunk" and trumpeting as you go, as everyone else sings Nelly The Elephant.

★ Give yourself a big behind by putting your pillow under your nightie/PJ bottoms, then ask each person in the room separately, "Does my bum look big in this?"

★ Pull the ugliest face you can, then pucker up and kiss the person of your choice.

★ Lie down while everyone tickles you for one minute.

★ Wriggle down into your sleeping bag, then pretend to be a beautiful butterfly emerging from your old caterpillar body, finishing by "flying" around the room singing, "Tra-la-la-la – ooh just look at my lovely wings!" over and over.

And now, Mate, after all that competitive business I think it's time you relaxed and treated yourselves to...

Makeovers and other pampering pastimes

One of the many great things about being a girl is that not only are you prettier than boys but you also get to spend hours making yourself even more gorgeous, at the same time as having a top laugh with your girl pals! (While boys just sit around being gawky and smelly with one another – we presume! Ha!) Anyway enough boy-talk, let's beautify! Mates, what've you got?

❝At Missy's last sleepover she did a manicure on each of us. All our nails looked amazing and we felt really glam. I think she should share her trade secrets with our Mate. Missy, how about it?**❞**

no probs, anything 4 our m8!

Missy's miracle five-minute manicure

You will need:

★ Soap ★ Moisturizer or hand cream ★ Nail file/emery board ★ Nail clippers/scissors ★ Nail varnish

What you do:

30 secs: soak hands in warm soapy water and dry.

10 secs: moisturize all over hands with the cream.

1 min 50 secs: trim nails and file into a gently rounded shape or a trendier, squarer shape (ask your "client" what she'd prefer) using a gentle stroke in one direction.

2 mins 30 secs: the tricky painting bit. Apply a small amount of polish to your brush. Paint one stroke down the centre of your nail, then use one stroke down each of the two sides of your nail. Bingo! Fab talons in no time!

fast or wot hey?! it's the same for yr feet, but remember 2 wedge cotton wool between yr toes 2 stop the varnish smudging – & it feels grrrr8! also try different colours (3 different stripes on 1 nail!) or buying some groovy nail transfers for yr guests.

Flower's Fruity face packs

66Try one of my home-made face packs. They get rid of all the dirt and grime from deep within your skin and leave you feeling really zingy!**99**

Lime and yoghurt

66This one cleanses and moisturizes oily skin.**99**

You will need:

★ One 5 ml spoon (one teaspoon) lime juice ★ One 5 ml spoon (one teaspoon) orange juice ★ Half a small carton plain yoghurt (unsweetened)

Mix ingredients together, smear on face and leave for five minutes. Then rinse off.

Banana and egg

❝This one nourishes the skin and tightens pores.**❞**

You will need:

★ One ripe banana ★ One egg yolk ★ Two 5 ml spoons (two teaspoons) of almond oil (optional)

Mix ingredients thoroughly with a fork. Splodge on face and rinse off after ten minutes.

❝While you're lying back waiting for your face pack to do its business, try plonking a couple of used, cold, damp tea bags or slices of cucumber on your (closed!) eyes – it takes away any puffiness and makes your eyes sparkle!**❞**

★ **Best Mates TOP TIP** ★

Create the effect of a beauty parlour by laying towels on a bed. Pick one or two of you to be pampered by the others; put on relaxing music and serve drinks from page 53 while your "clients" get their treatments.

❝This has all got far too girly! Where's the fun gone?!❞

Who says you can't be girly and have a laugh? Don't you remember when we did you up as that girl off EastEnders, Bubble? Which reminds me...

How to do celebrity makeovers

Once you're feeling all gorgeous and cleansed and your talons are looking dead sophisticated, it's time for some serious makeover action! Here's what to do:

1 Ask your guests to bring some make-up, hair accessories, flamboyant clothes and tons of recent magazines to the sleepover. Scrounge old make-up and stuff from your mum and her friends (women always have loads they never use). Tip everything you've got into a big pile on the floor.

2 Take a "before" photo of everyone. (If you don't have a camera get one of those disposable ones – with a built-in flash.)

3 Pick a partner – one of you is going to makeover the other one and vice versa.

4 Hunt through the magazines for pictures of the celeb your partner most wants to look like. Don't tell the others who you are doing.

5 Using your genius creative skills transform your partner – *Stars In Their Eyes* style – into their chosen celeb!

6 After everyone is finished, see if you can guess who everyone is supposed to be (if it's not immediately obvious who they are, turn it into a game by asking ten questions to which the "celeb" can only reply "yes" or "no").

7 Take your "after" pics – it'll make everyone feel very glam and will be hysterical comparing them to the before pictures when the film is developed!

A slight return to creative girly things

If you're anything like me or Flower – for example, a soppy sensitive type prone to blubbing over kittens, etc – my guess is you're the kind of girl who likes to have a reminder of brilliant events such as your fab sleepover.

Here are our two best ideas for utterly groovy, crafty things for you to make and keep.

Flower's Fabby Fun-Fur Flip-Flops

❝The fur-lining makes them feel super luxurious. They're so easy to make, even your dad could do it!!!**❞**

You will need:
★ A cheap pair of flip-flops ★ Fun fur (animal print, Day-Glo – whatever you fancy) ★ Sequins ★ Glue

What you do:
1 Place the flip-flops on the back of the fun fur. Draw around the bottoms of the flip-flops and cut out the shape in the fur, making sure you have one left foot and one right foot!
2 Take each fun-fur cut-out and, laying it over the correct flip-flop, use a pen to mark the three places where the strap joins the insole.
3 Now make a cut from the outer rim of the fun fur to where your pen marks are.

4 Smear each flip-flop's insole with glue, then carefully fix on your fun fur – it's easier if you start at the heel and roll the fun fur out up to the toe, adjusting it around the straps. The slits you made should now be hidden by the close fit of the insole and the shagginess of the fur!
5 Glue sequins along the straps and leave to dry.

* * * * * * * * * * * * * * * * * * *

Molly's groovily graffitied pillowcases

You will need:
★ A white pillowcase each ★ Bunch of fabric marker pens

What you do:
1 Each write the same slogan across the top of your pillowcase so you're united in your theme, something like: "I made it through a night with Missy, August 2004!"

g! thanx!

2 Personalize the pillowcase with a self-portrait, some in-jokes from your evening and get everyone to sign it. Then write goofy stuff on everyone else's.

Miscellaneous mucking about

Enough of the nice stuff, Mate. Now it's time we told you about some midnight monkey business!

66Ha ha! I like the sound of this!**99**

66I'm not sure I do – this stuff makes me nervous. We're not talking about anything too scary are we, Molly?**99**

Nah ... well, not yet, tee-hee! First, though, let's tell our Mate about our favourite pranks – a very traditional sleepover pastime.

The Best Mates' top five sleepover pranks

1 Put strips of bubble wrap between the toilet seat and the toilet rim. When your guest sits on the toilet she will be surprised by the, erm, "popping off" sound!

2 After the first girl has fallen asleep, everybody agree to convince her the next morning that she was talking in her sleep about her deep love for her chemistry teacher, the hideous Mr Stinkparp (or whoever you choose!).

3 Choose someone who's a heavy sleeper, then, once she's fast asleep, give her two big rosy dolly cheeks using an old lipstick. If she's a really heavy sleeper you could go for a curly-wurly moustache. Just make sure that whatever you use (eyeliner or facepaint) is easy to wash off.

4 Double wrap a big lump of cream cheese (or similar squishy stuff) in clingfilm and leave it where someone will tread on it when they get up in the morning. No harm will be done, but she won't think that at first!

5 Wait for the first person to fall asleep, then the rest of you waft a strong-smelling scent (perfume or deodorant) under her nose. In a whisper, ask your sleeping friend any question you want – she will give you a true answer in her sleep – and find out her deepest secrets!

66 Can I please tell our Mate about our latest versions of the traditional sleepover pillow fight? **99**

If you must, Bubs!

Bubble's boisterous variations on the pillow fight

Silly-string fight

Arm yourself with a silly-string canister and attack, attack, attack! (Probably best conducted outdoors, just in case Mum decides to, erm, nag, nag, nag!)

Balloon stomp

Given that you'll probably have loads of balloons around, it would seem a pity not to make good use of 'em! Simply tie a couple of balloons to everybody's ankles with a bit of string, then run around trying to burst everyone's balloons (using a stomping action only) before they get yours. Stomptastic fun!

And finally, Mate, after the scoff's been eaten, games played, pranks performed and makeovers, erm, madeover, darkness falls, an owl hoots in the distance and a floorboard creaks... Be scared, be very scared, 'cos it's...

Scary story time!

❝I wanna go h-h-home!❞

Aw, come on, Flower, it's practically compulsory to tell a few chilling stories at your sleepover. And, anyway, the Best Mates are nice girls – we're not in the business of distressing you or anyone else. Sleepovers are meant to be fun, so with that in mind and her sensible pants on, Princess has come up with the following rules:

Princess's code of conduct for (nicely) scaring each other

THE NUMBER ONE RULE: no scary films, seances or ouija board games. Not because the ghosties will come and get you, but because – with a little imagination and the excitement of the evening – you could become seriously freaked out and turn into a gibbering, babbling wreck. Not a good look for a girl.

THE NUMBER TWO RULE: no mean tricks that could lead a girl to think she was being hounded by a beast from hell. For instance, locking her out (too dangerous), picking on her, waking her in her sleep, etc.

Remember, keep the scary stories reasonably light.

You wanna still be able to laugh through those chattering teeth, right? I suggest you tell a few urban myth-type stories.

OK, Princess, let's give our Mate an idea of what kind of scary story is cool for sleepovers. Got one handy?

"I sure have. This is one I heard recently on the Internet. It goes something like this:**"**

The mysterious hitchhiker

Sally was 13 and on a holiday in America with her father, Sam. It was the first time they'd been away since the tragic death of Sally's mum, Teresa, the summer before. Her dad had thought it would be good to hire a car and just drive wherever the road took them. One dusky evening, as they were driving through the Arizona desert, with no sign of civilization for miles and miles, they saw a shadowy figure standing by the side of the road. As they drew closer, they saw it was a tall, bearded man with piercing eyes, who was holding out his thumb hitching a lift. Usually a cautious man, something made Sam stop and pick up the stranger. The man got into the car and just stared straight ahead. Even though Sam made loads of small talk, the man said nothing until he asked them to stop the car. Still in the middle of nowhere, Sam pulled over. The stranger turned to the father and daughter and simply said, "Teresa loves you both very much." He then got out of the car and when Sally and Sam looked back – he was gone. Seriously spooked, Sam reported the incident to the sheriff in the next town they came to. The sheriff sighed, and explained that it was the fifth time the mysterious hitcher had appeared that month, each time passing on a cryptic message before vanishing.

"Hang on ... was he a real person or a ghost?**"**

"A-ha! We may never know!**"**

So, Mate, have you got your sleepover superplan in place yet? Know what you're eating? Worked out your evening's entertainments? Whaddya mean, "No!"??? Oh dear, Mate, it sounds like you need the niggle-busting BMs to blast away your remaining poopy party problems! Let's move onwards to the next chapter and a worry-free sleepover world!

★

★

★ Your Sleepover Problems Sorted ★

Can't decide who to invite? Irksome brothers? Quarrelsome chums? We've been there... And now we're here to help you! Fire away, readers!

---

letter 1

Dad dread

Dear Best Mates

My name is Ella. I have tried everything I can think of to get my parents to let me have a sleepover, and they just say, "No. Out of the question." My dad says he doesn't want to be woken up all night and Mum just sides with him. The thing is, I've been to all my friends' houses and I'm now getting really embarrassed that I haven't been allowed to invite anyone back to mine. I'm dreading the next sleepover invite I get, knowing that I'm never going to be able to return the favour. What would you do?

Ella, 10, South London

What the Best Mates say

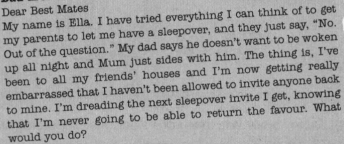

As your Best Mates, Ella, we must immediately assure you that we love and care for you and DO NOT judge you by your party-giving abilities! I'm sure your other friends wouldn't want you worrying about it either. If the old parent people are really set against a sleepover, try organizing one of the BMs girly gathering ideas from page 116 instead.

I'm always round Princess's or Missy's. I used to feel a bit guilty, but now I've come to accept that there are always going to be some girls who are better equipped (with bigger houses, more sympathetic parents, etc) to do the sleepover hostess thing. Enjoy being a guest – you get all the fun and none of the stress!

What about asking them if you can have one friend over to stay? Then invite one of your quieter, better-behaved friends for the night (someone nice like me, and not loud like Bubble!). See if that softens them to the idea of having a few of your friends over.

What the Best Mates say

Scary sleepover

Dear Best Mates
One of my friends, Lizzy, has invited me to her house for a Halloween sleepover. The thing is, she says we're going to do a seance, and I'm really scared. What should I do?

Laura, 12, Bridport

 Make your excuses and say you can't make it. You won't be missing out because scaring yourself stupid is not much fun. Besides, I'm sure you can find somewhere to go for a proper laugh on Halloween.

 have a quiet word with the other girls invited – I betcha some of them feel the same as U. then stand up for yourselves; say you'd love to come to her sleepover, but not if she's going 2 do scary stuff like that.

letter 3

Go away, Mum!

Dear Best Mates
My problem's my mum. I really love her and everything, and all my friends think she's great, it's just that she interferes all the time. If I have someone round she makes a big fuss – "Do they want a drink?", "Are they hungry?" etc – and if we're up in my room she'll waltz in and join in the conversation and stuff! Now she wants to organize a sleepover for my 11th birthday, and I'm kind of dreading it. What should I do?

May, 10, Cardiff

What the Best Mates say

Hmmm. The thing with having a cringey mum is that having friends who think she's great just makes it worse! The thing to do is to sit down with her and chat about this, but don't go blundering in telling her to keep her nose out (I mean, how would you feel if your mum took no notice of you?). Instead, discuss organizing your sleepover together and suggest she looks after food while you look after games. Then tell her you'll be playing "Truth or Dare" up in your room from 10 pm and that it's strictly out of bounds for parents. I'm sure she'll get the hint and, because you've included her in the earlier fun, she won't be offended.

Your mum sounds lovely! Let her get on with it!

Molly's right. You're going to have to include her a bit, or get a new mum!

letter 4

No mates!

Dear Best Mates
My name is Amy and I've just moved here from Glasgow. I've been at my new school for two weeks now but haven't made any friends yet. My mum suggested doing a sleepover. What do you think?

Amy, 11, Manchester

What the Best Mates say

Whoa there, Amy! Sleepovers are great fun with friends but you would be responsible for keeping happy what are practically strangers, like, all night. That's just way too much pressure – you'd be worrying what they thought of you all the time. And what if there was an argument or if it turned out that you didn't get on with one of the girls? A sleepover is too much to take on too soon.

Aw, Amy, it's horrible being the new girl, isn't it? But don't worry, you will make friends soon. I think it would be much better if you tried to join in what some of the other girls are up to. Ask one of the girls what she's doing at the weekend – see if she gets the hint and invites you along. And what about after-school stuff, like a drama group or a dance class? They're great ways of meeting new friends.

What the Best Mates say

Teddy or no teddy?
I always sleep with my teddy, Mr Poobah. Should I take him with me to my friend Tiffany's sleepover next week?

Mr Poobah's slightly embarrassed owner, 10, Norwich

I know loads of girls that have cuddly animals! And they can be particularly comforting if you're in a strange house. I always take Beareeno to the Mates' sleepovers, but I just slip him out of my bag and under the covers of my bed so no one sees him and takes the mickey!

i think u probably kno it's time u grew out of teddies – try going without him 4 this 1 night & see how u get on – u might surprise yourself! (& remember he'll b there when you get home!)

letter 6

Best mate stress
Dear Best Mates
Help! I'm having a sleepover on my birthday next month, but the problem is my best friend Sally. She's great fun but she's got a wicked streak. She always wants to do stuff like make prank phone calls and sneak out of the house and I'm getting really stressed that my parents are going to freak. I've tried asking her to promise not to do stuff, but she just laughs and calls me boring.

Anxious 12-year-old, Birmingham

What the Best Mates say

 Your mate Sally sounds like our Bubble! What we do with Bubble when she's on one of her "evil missions" is divert her attention by saying, "Hey, isn't it pizza time?" or putting on one of her pogo-tastic CDs really loudly. Just prepare yourself with some of the Best Mates' alternative entertainment ideas from the last chapter (Page 68).

 At the risk of sounding like a right girly swot, what about having a quiet word with your mum first? I'm sure she would happily take the blame for being the "party pooper" by making her house rules clear to your guests (see parents' tips on page 13) and secretly monitoring the front door and telephone for illegal usage. What's more, your friend need never know you've snitched on her!

letter 7

The 'b' word
Dear Best Mates
Is it ever acceptable to invite boys to a sleepover?

Debbie, 12, Essex

What the Best Mates say

 no waaaayyy! next!

I must back up Missy here. This is strictly a girly event, made for girls doing girly things. My brother (the ever-annoying Billy) is always bursting in when I've got the girls over "for a laugh" (did I tell you that he has a doughnut where his brain should be?) and it always causes much shrieking and distress. Girls simply do not want boys in their bedroom. Fact!

letter 8

Party pickle
Dear Best Mates
My name is Lily. I'm in a bit of a pickle about the sleepover I'm having next month. You see, I'm only allowed to invite three girls, but there's six of us that hang around together. I don't want to hurt anyone's feelings. What shall I do?

Lily, 11, London

▶

Invite the three girls you get on with best and explain separately to the others that you'd love to have invited them but numbers were limited. As they say, you can't please all of the people all of the time.

Try talking to your parents. Is there a way of making more space in your house (see our ideas on page 21). Could you camp out or borrow some bedding? Or could you invite everyone but only have a few girls to stay the night?

letter 9

Hanger on

Dear Best Mates

My little sister who's six is really annoying. Whenever I have a sleepover, she always hangs about following us and being a right pain in the bum. Help!

Angela, 10, Surrey

ship her out 2 tha grandprnts 4 the night but make it like she's getting a special treat. give her something u know she'd like – your fave hair scrunchy, a new colouring book – 4 going away with and being a good girl.

I've mentioned my seriously irksome twin Billy, haven't I? Mum knows how much he winds me and the Mates up, so she either tries to persuade him to stay the night at one of his pals, or she gets Dad to take him to the pictures. Either that or I bribe him to stay away. A bag of tortilla chips usually buys me about an hour of peace.

Aw, she's only little and trying to be like you! Be patient and tell her she can sit and watch but not interfere – just think how happy you'll make her.

Spooked out

Dear Best Mates

I was at a friend's sleepover recently when she got out a scary movie. I tried to say I didn't want to see it but I was in the minority, so I ended up watching it. I'm still having nightmares now. What would the Mates have done?

Spooked, 11, Edinburgh

What the Best Mates say

Well, first up, I think you need to do something about those nightmares. Tell your mum and/or dad what happened, let them know how troubled you are and I'm sure they can offer you reassurance. If you don't want to tell them, what about a school counsellor or friendly teacher? And remember, scary films are not real!

This is a real tough one. I'd have pointed out that it was against the law for us to be watching the film, and that I would be in serious trouble if my parents found out, and since my sensitive nature would mean I'd be well spooked (like your sweet self), and would probably suffer nightmares, the likelihood of them finding out was pretty high, and therefore I'd have to insist we didn't watch it. If my "friend" put it on anyway, I'd call my parents and ask to be picked up. I know it sounds a bit extreme but if someone tries to make you do something that will clearly distress you, then they're not that great a friend.

Girl trouble

Dear Best Mates

My problem is that my two best mates, Jenny and Fiona, are always arguing. They never agree on anything! And at Jenny's last sleepover they had a major argument and both ended up sulking for most of the night. Now I'm planning a sleepover and I'm worried that the same thing's going to happen. Any suggestions?

Sam (feeling like Mizz Piggy in the middle), 12, Cornwall

▶

Before your do, speak to each girl separately about your worries and ask them, as a personal favour to you, not to argue. If they do start arguing, supervise their row by standing between them, asking them to calm down and giving each girl a minute or two to make her point, during which time the other girl must be quiet. You must be relaxed, firm and strong. When both girls have had their say, offer a solution to the argument without taking sides with either girl.

Get them to have a fight! Seriously! One time me and Missy had a row that we settled by having a silly-string fight (see page 92). It was so crazy we just cracked up laughing and forgot all about our stupid squabble.

letter 12

A special something
Dear Best Mates
I'm planning my first major sleepover. I want it to be really special but can't think what to do. Any suggestions?

Jess, 11, Blackpool

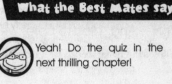

What the Best Mates say

Yeah! Do the quiz in the next thrilling chapter!

The Quiz

What kind of hostess are you? Which is the theme for you? Can you cope with party-prep stress? Do you make a good guest? Find out with our very revealing quiz!

Best Mates TOP TIP

For a laugh, try out our quiz on your chums on the night of your sleepover after lights out. Just remember to put this book, a pencil and torch by your bed and quiz away into the wee hours!

What kind of sleepover queen R U?

Tick one of the answers after each question, then turn to page 111, add up your scores and find your hostess profile. And, please note, we only accept honest answers here, Mate!

1 When was the last time you had friends (more than one) over to your house?

a) Within the last few days

b) About a week or so ago

c) Over a month ago

d) Over two weeks ago

e) The weekend just gone

2 Which word best describes you? (If you can't decide or are too bashful, ask a friend which one they think best suits you!)

a) Funny
b) Chatty
c) Caring
d) Cool
e) Laddy

3 When it comes to letting you have parties, what would best describe your parents' attitude?

a) They just let us get on with it
b) They have a whole list of rules, which they constantly go on about
c) Mum gets really excited – helping with the decorations and stuff – and Dad is pretty relaxed, making himself useful with little odd jobs
d) They're OK if there are just a few of us, but if things get loud they get a bit edgy
e) They're enthusiastic, which is great, but when they try to join in it can get a bit cringey!

4 Your idea of a good time with your mates is:
a) Scoffing pizzas and slurping cola

b) Staying up late, watching videos

c) Mucking about, making up games and winning prizes

d) Having a really good gossip

e) Having a luxurious pampering session

5 Which of the following places and time periods would you most enjoy?

a) London in the groovy 1960s – all those fab clothes and wild parties with amazing celebrities

b) The next century – when we each have our own spaceship parked in the drive and pop off to a theme-park planet for fun!

c) The nineteenth century in the Wild West of America – riding horses around amazing scenery all day and looking dead cool

d) Egypt a couple of thousand years back – making like Queen Cleopatra, being pampered all day and living in incredible palaces

e) Some time when there's no hunger and there are no wars going on

6 You are holding a karaoke competition and you fail to win first prize. What's your reaction?

a) Right, like you'd be bothered by *that*

b) A bit gutted, you know you sing really well

c) To get on with the next game as soon as possible

d) You're really happy for the person who's won

e) Slightly disappointed but also happy for the winner

7 Which of these statements best describes your sleeping habits?

a) I like to stay up late but get a bit groggy if I don't get a good ten hours kip

b) I sometimes find it hard to go to sleep

c) I love to sleep and nod off really easily

d) I often stay awake half the night!

e) I usually like a lie-in, especially at weekends

8 You're having a sleepover when two of your friends start having a big dispute about something. Things are getting a bit heated. What do you do?

a) Try to settle it by offering your opinion on whatever they're arguing about

b) Remain calm and try to direct their argument towards an agreement

c) Let them argue it out between them

d) Try and distract them by starting a fun game

e) Tell both parties how much they are stressing you out, and ask them to stop. Now!

9 Do you worry about what other people think about you and where you live?
a) If I'm honest, yes, quite a lot
b) Fairly often – it's nice to be liked!
c) Very rarely
d) Not when they're good friends
e) Never

10 Which of these statements most accurately describes the current state of your bedroom?
a) A cool hang-out with your telly and stereo taking pride of place
b) Hmmm … you've been meaning to tidy it for a few days now – so it's a bit messy, with your homework scattered about and your stinky trainers in the corner, otherwise it's pretty average: posters, bed, computer, etc…
c) Stylish, with a dressing table full of interesting clutter and a wardrobe crammed with clothes and stuff
d) An adult-free zone, littered with lots of crazy stuff, loads of posters on the walls – and a few heaps of clothes here and there

e) Cosy and relaxing – lots of stuffed teddies on the bed, full of interesting knick-knacks everywhere

Now work out your scores!

Question 1	a = 1	b = 4	c = 5	d = 2	e = 3
Question 2	a = 4	b = 1	c = 2	d = 3	e = 5
Question 3	a = 3	b = 5	c = 1	d = 2	e = 4
Question 4	a = 5	b = 3	c = 4	d = 1	e = 2
Question 5	a = 1	b = 3	c = 5	d = 2	e = 4
Question 6	a = 3	b = 1	c = 5	d = 2	e = 4
Question 7	a = 4	b = 5	c = 2	d = 3	e = 1
Question 8	a = 5	b = 2	c = 3	d = 4	e = 1
Question 9	a = 1	b = 2	c = 3	d = 4	e = 5
Question 10	a = 3	b = 4	c = 1	d = 5	e = 2

If you scored under 18: Ooh-la-la lady!

Ups: You are mature, super confident and pride yourself on having good taste in all things. What's more you have the potential to be one of the best sleepover hostesses ever!

Downs: Although hugely talented, you can be an overly competitive hostess – try to let your guests share a bit of the limelight!

You are most like: Princess
Recommended theme: Glittery disco
Top pursuits: Karaoke competitions and late-night gossiping

If you scored 18–25: Laid-back lassie!

Ups: You are passionate, love to have fun, possess a truly giving spirit and like nothing better than to be part of a happy gang. You make a very kind and generous host.

Downs: You can be a bit wimpy at times, but if you want your sleepover to run smoothly you must learn to take charge and organize things yourself.

You are most like: Flower
Recommended theme: Exotic East
Top pursuits: Giant sundae-making, pampering and makeovers

If you scored 26–33: Hang-out honey!

Ups: Everyone wants to come to your place 'cos,

besides being super trendy, you are also fiercely loyal to your friends, love a laugh, are refreshingly honest, intelligent and make a mega-chilled hostess.

Downs: Sometimes you can be a bit too cool and, because you have everyone round so much, you don't always make a big effort. Try to do something a little different each time you entertain and make sure you always find time to talk to your guests individually to let them know you appreciate them being there.

You are most like: Missy

Recommended theme: Hollywood glamour

Top pursuits: Checking out the latest movies and late-night pranks

If you scored 34–41: The giggler

Ups: You adore your friends, love acting the fool, are witty, wise and make a natural leader. All in all, you are a confident and very capable hostess.

Downs: You put so much effort into trying to get everything right that you sometimes forget to enjoy yourself. So what if no one wants to do something you've arranged? And what's the big deal if your mum gets involved? Stop being a control freak and go with the flow!

You are most like: Molly

Recommended theme:
None (you don't have to
have one, y'know!)

Top pursuits: Making yummy
snacks and playing late-night
Truth or Dare

If you scored over 41: Ms Va-Va-Voom!

Ups: Slightly bonkers, full of life, very excitable and thrilling to be around – that's you! Plus you make an excellent guest – always enthusiastic and a magnificent spreader of good vibes.

Downs: Your scatty nature (and possibly your worry-wart parents) means that your hosting skills are a bit, erm, basic. You need to calm down and think about what your guests might want to do, rather than rushing about like a mad thing.

You are most like: Bubble

Recommended theme: Cowboy camp-out

Top pursuits: Pizza-making and chilling out watching a late-night film

Almost goodbye!

The time has come, dear fellow Best Mate, for you to venture out into the sleepover world by yourself (sob!). And, y'know, I'm kinda confident that you are going to make a totally happening sleepover hostess. BUT, before we go, it occurred to me and the rest of the BMs that we should mention a few of our other fave things to do in our girl gang when not having sleepovers. So, seekers of girly gathering fun, read on and prepare for yet more merriment...

Some Other Girly Gathering Ideas

"This sounds impressive! Have *we* done all these?**"**

2 right we hve!

"I think it should be every Mate's ambition to have done at least, like, ten of them before teenagedom strikes!**"**

A fine idea, Princess! OK, Mate, let's make a pact: tick each girly gathering off as you've done it. When you've scored a magical ten, you get to become an honorary life member of the Best Mates – forever respected, loved and clasped to the BMs' metaphorical bosom!

❝Steady on, Moll!❞

Right, let's get, ahem, ticking!

☐ Have a mad bad hair day

Meet up in a friend's bedroom and give yourselves the freakiest hairstyles possible. For a spiky, bush effect, pump on lashings of hairspray and then backcomb (use a comb, making small movements from the tips to the roots). Then, for extra punkdom, add some temporary-colour spray (available quite cheaply from larger chemists), feathers, cheapo tiaras and whatever else you fancy.

☐ Make like ice fairies at the skate rink

Go to your nearest ice rink (check on the Internet or in the telephone directory to find one) and zip around in a blur of elegance and furry ear muffs.

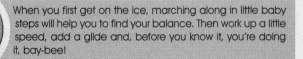

Best Mates TOP TIP

When you first get on the ice, marching along in little baby steps will help you to find your balance. Then work up a little speed, add a glide and, before you know it, you're doing it, bay-bee!

❑ Intimidate everyone at the bowling alley

Going bowling is brilliant fun, not that expensive and really easy to learn.

❑ Scoff sweets and weep!

There's no better way to cheer up a miserable friend than a bunch of girlies getting together and indulging in a little chocolate therapy – then letting it all out (your emotional probs, not the choc, that is!).

❝For supreme chocolatey comfort, top a mug of hot chocolate with a handful of mini marshmallows and spray cream – who could carry on being sad with that in their hands?!**❞**

❑ Become backyard beachbabes

Let the beach come to you and your friends on a sunny day. Put on your cozzie, shades, grab the sun cream, a big bunch of glossy mags and lounge round your little sister's paddling pool (well, a girl needs somewhere to cool her tootsies).

❝For the ultimate in sun-chick sophistication, sip one of my smoothies (see page 54) poured over ice in a tall glass.❞

☐ Head for the fearground! Er, sorry, fairground

Persuade a parent to take you and the girlfriends to a theme park, vote on which of the scary big rides you all dare go on – then prepare to SCRRREEEEEMMM!!!! as you hurtle towards Jupiter at a gubillion miles an hour with everyone looking up at your knickers.

Best Mates
TOP TIP

Save the hot dogs and candyfloss for after the ride ... unless you want to meet Rrrralf and his sister Berrrtha (ho ho)!

☐ Form a fashion-design studio

Get all your pals to gather a bunch of old clothes – especially jeans and other denim stuff – and loads of sewing materials (scissors, threads, patches, sequins, fake gemstones, fabric paint and glue, etc) and hole up in a bedroom for an evening designing an outfit each.

go mad ripping & slashing with the scissors (careful tho!) – the distressed look is sooo in!

❑ Pretend you're a hot new pop act

Grab a copy of the lyrics of a catchy song by a new girl band (some of the CDs come with lyrics, otherwise check out the teen mags) and get together with your mates to learn your parts. Then, when out in public, burst into "spontaneous" renditions of your "hit".

Best Mates
TOP TIP

Say stuff like, "Ooh, I've had enough of rehearsals today" and "I hope no one recognizes us, I'm tired..." for that authentic moany pop star imitation.

❑ Make like a cool skateboard park punk

Transform yourselves into skateheads by pushing your jeans down to hip level (while pulling your pants upwards, so the tops are showing), putting on your baggiest tee, scruffiest trainers and backwards baseball cap, then heading off to the park.

Don't worry if you can't actually skateboard, instead perfect a cool walk – slouch your shoulders, swagger and make hip-hop-style hand signals when you talk (gesture with both your thumb and pinky). Cooo-el!

☐ The pizza pilgrimage

There are times in every girl's life when all she needs is a pizza restaurant and the company of good friends to be in absolute heaven. Awww.

❝All agree to get really glammed-up for your trip out – it'll make it much more special.❞

☐ Become a cyber gang

Arrange to meet in a chat room on a certain day at a certain time. Before you go online, invent cyber aliases for yourselves and devise some sort of secret code that only you know.

here's some txt slang we Mates always use:

BCNU	– be seeing you
ESOSL	– endless snorts of stupid laughter
GGP	– gotta go pee
HHOJ	– ha ha only joking
L8R	– later!
M8	– mate!
ZAM	– zzz's are me (ie, bedtime!)
ZZZOVA	– sleepover!

❑ Come up with your own cheerleader routine

Get together to learn the following basic moves and put them together with a few high kicks, jumps and a chant:

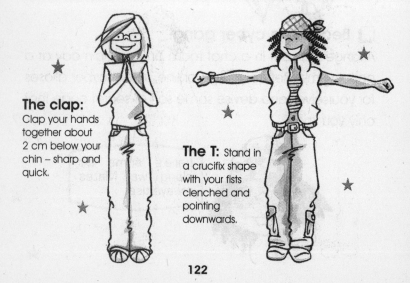

The clap:
Clap your hands together about 2 cm below your chin – sharp and quick.

The T: Stand in a crucifix shape with your fists clenched and pointing downwards.

The goalpost:
Stand with your arms raised straight up, touching the sides of your head, again clenching your fists.

Cone head:
From the goalpost position, unclench your fists and clap your hands together.

High V: From the goalpost position, widen your arms so your body forms a V.

Low V: This time, for an upside-down V, move your arms straight down by your sides.

The chant: The idea is to get the crowd cheering with you. Try the traditional ones like: "Give me an S (crowd: S!). Give me an P (crowd: P!). Give me an A (crowd: A!). Give me an M (crowd: M!). Whaddya got? (Crowd: SPAM!!!!!)" You become a mad jumping thing at this point.

66 Show off your new-found skills at a major local sporting event. Go on, dare you to do it at the next important school footie match! 2–4–6–8 Who do we appreciate? Spamshire Secondary FC!!!! 99

❏ Shop! Shop! Shop!

Is there a better place for a girl to be than a changing room on a Saturday afternoon, with a few quid in her pocket, trying on a selection of the trendiest garments imaginable, and a bunch of her tittering, bestest pals telling her that she looks simply divine? No. There is not!

❝Don't underestimate the joy of the mini shopping trip. Even if you're short on funds, finding the most bargainous beaded choker can still be a chuckle-filled and uplifting mission.**❞**

❏ Go sport mad followed by a pig-out picnic

Summery kinda day? Grab a bat, ball, plenty of munchies and head for the park! Try a game of rounders or, if there aren't that many of you, chuck a frisbee around (while chewing your gum, naturally – you don't want to look as though you're making *too* much effort).

Best Mates
TOP TIP

Frustrated? Annoyed? Parents on your case? Schoolwork getting you down? Let it all out by thwacking that ball as hard as you can, Mate!

❏ Experience some big-screen action

It's gotta be a mega blockbuster, with eardrum-rattling stereo surround-sound, a humungous carton of popcorn, giant vat of slurpy drink and, of course, your bezzie mates at your side. Kinda like having your eyeballs rocket out of your head and orbit round the moon a couple of times before plopping back into your sockets, a trip to the cinema should leave you totally inspired and refreshed!

head 4 fast-food joint L8R – essential 4 a proper chat about what you all thought about the film.

We really are going this time…

And so, with a big lump in our throats we Best Mates must say goodbye to you, our newest Mate … but only for now! 'Cos we've got loads more to share with you. So, hopefully see you soon,

Lots of hugs,

★

Molly
x

L8r Missy ☺

Just remember,
you are the best!
Princess xx

★

We'll be
thinking of ya!!
Flower xxxx

★

And, hey, hope you have the best
sleepovers ever! Bubble! ooo

★

Get more great advice from

The best mates...